Youths tragedy a poem, drawn up by way of dialogue between youth, the Devil, wisdom, time, death, the soul, the nuncius: for the caution and direction of the younger sort. (1672)

T. S

Youths tragedy a poem, drawn up by way of dialogue between youth, the Devil, wisdom, time, death, the soul, the nuncius : for the caution and direction of the younger sort.
Youth undone.
T. S.
[Edition statement:] The third edition /by T.S.
Attributed to Thomas Sherman. Cf. NUC pre-1956.
Published in 1709 as: Youth undone.
"Licensed and entred according to order"
[2], 30 p.
London : Printed for John Starkey ... and Francis Smith ...,
Arber's Term cat. / I 107
Wing / S3393
English
Reproduction of the original in the Henry E. Huntington Library and Art Gallery

Early English Books Online (EEBO) Editions

Imagine holding history in your hands.

Now you can. Digitally preserved and previously accessible only through libraries as Early English Books Online, this rare material is now available in single print editions. Thousands of books written between 1475 and 1700 and ranging from religion to astronomy, medicine to music, can be delivered to your doorstep in individual volumes of high-quality historical reproductions.

We have been compiling these historic treasures for more than 70 years. Long before such a thing as "digital" even existed, ProQuest founder Eugene Power began the noble task of preserving the British Museum's collection on microfilm. He then sought out other rare and endangered titles, providing unparalleled access to these works and collaborating with the world's top academic institutions to make them widely available for the first time. This project furthers that original vision.

These texts have now made the full journey -- from their original printing-press versions available only in rare-book rooms to online library access to new single volumes made possible by the partnership between artifact preservation and modern printing technology. A portion of the proceeds from every book sold supports the libraries and institutions that made this collection possible, and that still work to preserve these invaluable treasures passed down through time.

This is history, traveling through time since the dawn of printing to your own personal library.

Initial Proquest EEBO Print Editions collections include:

Early Literature

This comprehensive collection begins with the famous Elizabethan Era that saw such literary giants as Chaucer, Shakespeare and Marlowe, as well as the introduction of the sonnet. Traveling through Jacobean and Restoration literature, the highlight of this series is the Pollard and Redgrave 1475-1640 selection of the rarest works from the English Renaissance.

Early Documents of World History

This collection combines early English perspectives on world history with documentation of Parliament records, royal decrees and military documents that reveal the delicate balance of Church and State in early English government. For social historians, almanacs and calendars offer insight into daily life of common citizens. This exhaustively complete series presents a thorough picture of history through the English Civil War.

Historical Almanacs

Historically, almanacs served a variety of purposes from the more practical, such as planting and harvesting crops and plotting nautical routes, to predicting the future through the movements of the stars. This collection provides a wide range of consecutive years of "almanacks" and calendars that depict a vast array of everyday life as it was several hundred years ago.

Early History of Astronomy & Space

Humankind has studied the skies for centuries, seeking to find our place in the universe. Some of the most important discoveries in the field of astronomy were made in these texts recorded by ancient stargazers, but almost as impactful were the perspectives of those who considered their discoveries to be heresy. Any independent astronomer will find this an invaluable collection of titles arguing the truth of the cosmic system.

Early History of Industry & Science

Acting as a kind of historical Wall Street, this collection of industry manuals and records explores the thriving industries of construction; textile, especially wool and linen; salt; livestock; and many more.

Early English Wit, Poetry & Satire

The power of literary device was never more in its prime than during this period of history, where a wide array of political and religious satire mocked the status quo and poetry called humankind to transcend the rigors of daily life through love, God or principle. This series comments on historical patterns of the human condition that are still visible today.

Early English Drama & Theatre

This collection needs no introduction, combining the works of some of the greatest canonical writers of all time, including many plays composed for royalty such as Queen Elizabeth I and King Edward VI. In addition, this series includes history and criticism of drama, as well as examinations of technique.

Early History of Travel & Geography

Offering a fascinating view into the perception of the world during the sixteenth and seventeenth centuries, this collection includes accounts of Columbus's discovery of the Americas and encompasses most of the Age of Discovery, during which Europeans and their descendants intensively explored and mapped the world. This series is a wealth of information from some the most groundbreaking explorers.

Early Fables & Fairy Tales

This series includes many translations, some illustrated, of some of the most well-known mythologies of today, including Aesop's Fables and English fairy tales, as well as many Greek, Latin and even Oriental parables and criticism and interpretation on the subject.

Early Documents of Language & Linguistics

The evolution of English and foreign languages is documented in these original texts studying and recording early philology from the study of a variety of languages including Greek, Latin and Chinese, as well as multilingual volumes, to current slang and obscure words. Translations from Latin, Hebrew and Aramaic, grammar treatises and even dictionaries and guides to translation make this collection rich in cultures from around the world.

Early History of the Law

With extensive collections of land tenure and business law "forms" in Great Britain, this is a comprehensive resource for all kinds of early English legal precedents from feudal to constitutional law, Jewish and Jesuit law, laws about public finance to food supply and forestry, and even "immoral conditions." An abundance of law dictionaries, philosophy and history and criticism completes this series.

Early History of Kings, Queens and Royalty

This collection includes debates on the divine right of kings, royal statutes and proclamations, and political ballads and songs as related to a number of English kings and queens, with notable concentrations on foreign rulers King Louis IX and King Louis XIV of France, and King Philip II of Spain. Writings on ancient rulers and royal tradition focus on Scottish and Roman kings, Cleopatra and the Biblical kings Nebuchadnezzar and Solomon.

Early History of Love, Marriage & Sex

Human relationships intrigued and baffled thinkers and writers well before the postmodern age of psychology and self-help. Now readers can access the insights and intricacies of Anglo-Saxon interactions in sex and love, marriage and politics, and the truth that lies somewhere in between action and thought.

Early History of Medicine, Health & Disease

This series includes fascinating studies on the human brain from as early as the 16th century, as well as early studies on the physiological effects of tobacco use. Anatomy texts, medical treatises and wound treatment are also discussed, revealing the exponential development of medical theory and practice over more than two hundred years.

Early History of Logic, Science and Math

The "hard sciences" developed exponentially during the 16th and 17th centuries, both relying upon centuries of tradition and adding to the foundation of modern application, as is evidenced by this extensive collection. This is a rich collection of practical mathematics as applied to business, carpentry and geography as well as explorations of mathematical instruments and arithmetic; logic and logicians such as Aristotle and Socrates; and a number of scientific disciplines from natural history to physics.

Early History of Military, War and Weaponry

Any professional or amateur student of war will thrill at the untold riches in this collection of war theory and practice in the early Western World. The Age of Discovery and Enlightenment was also a time of great political and religious unrest, revealed in accounts of conflicts such as the Wars of the Roses.

Early History of Food

This collection combines the commercial aspects of food handling, preservation and supply to the more specific aspects of canning and preserving, meat carving, brewing beer and even candy-making with fruits and flowers, with a large resource of cookery and recipe books. Not to be forgotten is a "the great eater of Kent," a study in food habits.

Early History of Religion

From the beginning of recorded history we have looked to the heavens for inspiration and guidance. In these early religious documents, sermons, and pamphlets, we see the spiritual impact on the lives of both royalty and the commoner. We also get insights into a clergy that was growing ever more powerful as a political force. This is one of the world's largest collections of religious works of this type, revealing much about our interpretation of the modern church and spirituality.

Early Social Customs

Social customs, human interaction and leisure are the driving force of any culture. These unique and quirky works give us a glimpse of interesting aspects of day-to-day life as it existed in an earlier time. With books on games, sports, traditions, festivals, and hobbies it is one of the most fascinating collections in the series.

The BiblioLife Network

This project was made possible in part by the BiblioLife Network (BLN), a project aimed at addressing some of the huge challenges facing book preservationists around the world. The BLN includes libraries, library networks, archives, subject matter experts, online communities and library service providers. We believe every book ever published should be available as a high-quality print reproduction; printed on-demand anywhere in the world. This insures the ongoing accessibility of the content and helps generate sustainable revenue for the libraries and organizations that work to preserve these important materials.

The following book is in the "public domain" and represents an authentic reproduction of the text as printed by the original publisher. While we have attempted to accurately maintain the integrity of the original work, there are sometimes problems with the original work or the micro-film from which the books were digitized. This can result in minor errors in reproduction. Possible imperfections include missing and blurred pages, poor pictures, markings and other reproduction issues beyond our control. Because this work is culturally important, we have made it available as part of our commitment to protecting, preserving, and promoting the world's literature.

GUIDE TO FOLD-OUTS MAPS and OVERSIZED IMAGES

The book you are reading was digitized from microfilm captured over the past thirty to forty years. Years after the creation of the original microfilm, the book was converted to digital files and made available in an online database.

In an online database, page images do not need to conform to the size restrictions found in a printed book. When converting these images back into a printed bound book, the page sizes are standardized in ways that maintain the detail of the original. For large images, such as fold-out maps, the original page image is split into two or more pages

Guidelines used to determine how to split the page image follows:

- Some images are split vertically; large images require vertical and horizontal splits.
- For horizontal splits, the content is split left to right.
- For vertical splits, the content is split from top to bottom.
- For both vertical and horizontal splits, the image is processed from top left to bottom right.

D
S 3393

147750

REPRODUCED FROM THE COPY IN THE

HENRY E. HUNTINGTON LIBRARY

FOR REFERENCE ONLY, NOT FOR REPRODUCTION

Youths Tragedy,

A

POEM:

Drawn up by way of Dialogue between

{ *Youth.* *Time.* }
{ *The Devil.* *Death.* }
{ *Wisdom.* *The Soul.* }
The *Nuncius.*

For the Caution, and Direction, of the Younger Sort.

Frange toros, pete vina, rosas cape, tingere nardo,
Fræna voluptati laxa, tua tempora vanæ
Lætitiæ voveas, tamen hoc sub mente revolvas,
Divinam ad Stygias Nemesin te poscere pœnas.

Ψυχὴ δ' ἐκ ῥεθέων πταμένη, ἄϊδός δε βεβήκει
Ὃν πότμον γοόωσα, λιποῦσ' ἀδροτῆτα καὶ ἥβην.

Hom.

The Third Edition by *T. S.*

Licensed and Entred according to Order.

LONDON,
Printed for *John Starkey* at the *Mitre* in *Fleetstreet*, near *Temple-Barr*, and *Francis Smith* at the *Castle* and *Elephant* without *Temple-Barr*. 1672.

The Speakers.

Youth.   Time.
The Devil.   Death.
Wisdom.   The Soul.
The *Nuncius.*

The Argument.

1. Scene.   The first Scene shews, how Youth with self consults,
And, from depraved Nature, what results.

2. Sc.   How Satan suits his Bait, and deadly Snare
To Youthful Lust, the next Scene doth declare.

3. Sc.   The third, how Wisdom labours for to win
To Paths of life, from the ensnaring Gin;
And answers what objections do arise,
Scaling those works, where Youth insconced lies.

4. Sc.   What great Convictions hereupon possess
The Young-man's Soul, the fourth Scene doth express.

5. Sc.   How they wear off, and how he hardned grows,
By fresh Satanick Wiles, the fifth Scene showes.

6. Sc.   Floting in Mirth, swelling with Scoffing pride,
The sixth Scene doth the sinful Youth describe.

7, 8, 9. Sc.   In the three next, swift Time, and meager Death,
Periods his days, and spoileth all his mirth.

10. Sc.   Within the tenth doth his Tormented Soul,
Slighted advice, and mis-spent Time condole.

11. Sc.   With offers of rich Grace and sweet Repose
Unto the living, doth the last Scene close.

Youths Tragedie,
A POEM:

Drawn up

By way of Dialogue for the Caution and Direction of the Younger Sort.

The Prologue.

If thou art serious, then attend, and see,
If not, yet stay, that thou maist serious be.
And whil'st thou view'st, consider that thou art
No bare spectator, but dost act a part.
And as thou shalt within these Scenes engage,
So must thou fare, when Time pulls down the stage.

Youth.

How pleasant is it, when the Sun displays,   1.S
From *Aries*'s Golden Fleece, his Golden Rays?
How do the Creatures triumph for to see,
Imprison'd *Nature* set at libertie?
How doth the *Earth* rejoyce, that she is seen
Cloath'd in a rich imbroider'd *Vest* of Green.

A 2   *Verna*

Youths Tragedy.

Verna now wakens *Flora* from her bed,
And being up, adorns her lovely head.
Sweet *Flora* smiles, to see her self so fair,
And comes abroad for to perfume the Air.
Aurora mantled with the beams of light
Early sets forth to chase away the night.
Phœbus soon rouzeth, from the Ocean streams,
To influence our World with fruitful beams:
And as with Glory, he the Heaven spreads,
The twinkling *Lamps* outshin'd, withdraw their heads.
The Heavens are pleasant darksom Clouds do flie,
And give a Prospect of an Azur'd Skie;
From Dewie turf the towring *Lark* ascends,
And with choice Layes, upon the Morn attends.
The pretty winged Quire, from their sweet throats
Fill every place with their Melodious Notes.

And what is *Youth* ? but like another Spring,
And therefore Young man, now rejoyce and sing.
Discharge sad thoughts, follow thy Recreation,
Whil'st that thy Blood hath a free circulation.
Let Old *Barzillaies* now refuse the Court,
Thy nimble parts adapted are for sport:
Let thy heart chear thee, and now chuse delight,
According as thine Eye shall thee invite.

The *Devil* and *Youth*.

Scene

Devil. Bravely resolv'd, give up thy strength, an
To please thy self, and all things shall be thine. (tim

Youths Tragedy.

Go view from *Southern* to the *Artick* Pole,
The glory over which the Heavens do role,
And make thy choice; when done, put forth thy hand,
And please thy self, it's all at thy command.
Riches shall at thy Feet full Bags fling down,
And give a Golden Chain, and Scarlet Gown :
Honour will quickly court thee, and shall set
Upon thy Head, a Golden Coronet :
Pleasure shall strow thy paths with Fragrant Flowers,
And Solace thee within her Shady Bowers ;
Only this word of Counsel, must thee guide,
Trouble thy Head with nothing else beside.

Youth. I'le take thy Counsel, *Conscience* now adieu,
I see I shall have little need of you :
I am resolv'd to suffer no controul,
But to pursue these things with all my *Soul.*

Wisdom and *Youth.*

Wisdom. Pursue with all thy *Soul,* nay fond *Youth* 3. Scene
And view the Lie, that's lodg'd in thy right hand: (stand,
He that these great things to thee doth propose,
Is free to promise what he cann't dispose ;
Neither canst thou acquire, with all thy haste,
Far lesser things, if *God* endeavours blast.
But grant thou had'st what's promis'd, yet thy mind
Instead of *Joy,* would but *Vexation* find :
Inlarg'd desires, will keep thee from *Content,*
And what can't satisfie, will but *Torment.*

B ut

But could the *World* compleat *Joy* to thee bring,
Yet at the best, it's but a transient thing:
These *Worldly* things which thou enjoy'st to day,
To morrow may take Wings, and fly away.
Thy Soul's Immortal, look what doth agree
Unto its *Nature*, that must Satiate thee;
There's nought but the great *Fountain Good* that will
Suit with thy *Soul*, and thy vast *Spirit* fill.
Come then, and tread those paths that will thee bring
Unto the everlasting flowing *Spring*
Of pure, unmixed, intellectual *Joyes*;
Why should'st thou cheat thy self with empty *Toyes*.

   Youth. The way is Long, and Thorny that doth lead
Unto these *Joyes*, and those that do it tread,
Water their Steps with Tears, and break their Rest
With those sad Sighs and Groans which fill their Breast.
Wormwood, and *Gall*, on each side of it grow,
Crosses, and *Jears*, this dolorous way do strow,
And all along this Path you may espie,
Here scat'red a right Hand, there a right Eye,
Here a dear Lust, there a dead Comfort lies,
By *Self-denial* made a Sacrifice;
And on the Hills do fired Beacons flame,
Which round about, invading *Foes* proclaim:
To whom I either must become a Prey,
Or through their Hostile Troops must fight my way.
Pardon me then, if that I do refuse,
Such *Doleful Wayes* of Trouble, for to chuse.

                                            Wisdom.

Wisdom. Though at the first, this *Way* may seem to be
A Thornie, Rough, Unpleasant Path to thee,
Yet do but try it, what at first seems hard,
Will easie prove unto thee afterward.
For when thy heart, shall be enlarg'd with love,
Unto those glorious things which are above;
Then wilt thou run these ways with great delight,
For in them there is strength to the upright.

Let not those Tears affright thee that are spent
The future *Floods* of sorrow to prevent:
No Wine so precious, as what doth arise,
From the sweet springs of penitential eyes;
No frame like this, where comfort doth so thrive,
For *God* the contrite Spirit doth revive.

Nor let it daunt thee, that thou must deny
Thy *Youthful Lusts*, and dear self *Mortifie*;
The blessed end is, that thou may'st *Destroy*
Those *Succors* that would hinder thy true *Joy*,
And whil'st thou conflicts thus, and giv'st the *Foil*,
Thou'lt sing with those that do divide the *Spoil*.

Let not the *Cross* dismay thee, God will fit
It to thy Back, or thy Back unto it.
And what affliction, he doth to thee measure,
It's for thy profit, and not for his pleasure,
That with more even steps thy *Soul* may press,
Forward unto its final happiness.

Fear not to Fight, the Conquest shall be sure,
To him that doth unto the End endure;

For

For by a Hand of Strength, he shall be led
Upon the Necks of all his *Foes* to tread.
And on a *Throne* of *Glory* shall sit down
With songs of *Praise*, and a triumphant *Crown*.

   Call not these Paths then *Dolesom, Youngman* cease,
All *Wisdom's Ways* are *Pleasantness* and *Peace*.
Whilst a good *Conscience* lodgeth in thy Breast,
Thou need'st not doubt of a continual Feast.
Ask those that follow *Wisdom*, and they'l say,
They feed on hidden *Manna* in their way:
By acts of *Faith*, and *Love* they now possess
That inward Sweetness, which they cann't express.
Strong *Consolations* here do fill their *Cup*,
Whil'st with eternal *Love* their Souls do Sup.

   Youth. I understand not how these *Joys* commence,
Youth must have something that may please the sense;
Therefore forbear until thou offer'st that,
Which may be suited to my present State.

   Wisdom. Fond *Youth*, thou know'st not what is true (delight,
It's not to please the sensual *Appetite* :
This will debase thy *Nature*, and the *Fruit*
Will be to lay thee level with the *Brute*.
That which ennobles, and doth truly raise,
Are *Visions* of those *Beams* which *God* displays,
From his sweet reconciled *Face*, which make
The *Soul* of his bless'd *Nature* to partake.

   Youth. These are but darksom *Riddles*, canting *streins*
Fitted to suit with *Melancholy* Veins :

Wha

What canst thou offer now unto my *Eye*,
That will the *Glory* of this *World* outvie?

 Wisdom. Whil'st thou a darksom *Riddle* this dost call,
Thou show'st thy woful Darkness since the fall,
For though an instinct still remains to *Bliss*,
Yet wantest Light to guide thee where it is.
And whil'st thou counts my words as canting *Streins*,
Thou shew'st what Rancor in thy *Nature* Reigns;
Which is so far invelop'd in dark night,
As that like Death it hates the beams of Light.

 But will the good things of this world content?
Then view what *Wisdom* doth of this present:
Honour and *Riches* her left hand enfolds,
And in her right hand length of days she holds;
Which she gives forth to them that do her love,
So far as they may real blessings prove:
If what thou hast be mixed with a curse,
It will prove to thee *Vanity*, nay, worse.
That hand of *Mercy* that gives forth the Treasure,
To make it Mercy, must give forth the Measure;
That hand must guide thee how it must be us'd;
Mercies prove *Judgments* when they are abus'd.
Take all thy good things then from *Wisdoms* hand,
And use those good things as she doth command.

 Youth. If *Wisdom's* ways so eligible are,
Why do so few unto her paths repair?
And those from thatched Roof, and Fishers boat,
Why not the Wise, the Great, and men of Note?

      B   Such

Such as the bright Celestial bodies measure,
And their vast distances, can tell at Pleasure,
That know the Motion of the Heavenly Sphears,
And how the wandring Planets, in them Stears;
When they progressive are, and when they stray,
Why do they not discover this same way?
   The mighty Agonist that spends his days
In great Atchievements, for a wreath of Bays,
That courts forth Danger, for to raise Renown,
Why don't he strive, for the Immortal Crown?
   The Rich man, that from Mountains of thick clay
Doth take a prospect, jointly for to lay
Houses and Lands, great Lordships for to rear,
Why do not such men, make a purchase here?
   The high born Noble, whose vast thought aspires,
To rise in honour to the twinkling Fires;
Whose Grandeur wants more Worlds to make him (room,
Why seeks he not this World that is to come?

Wisd. If *Wisdom's* followers, with the World's thou (view,
It is acknowledg'd then, they are but few,
For most with present sensual things converse,
And in their drossy Lusts, their souls immerse.
Yet if thou wilt but view in sacred story,
The Multitudes before the Throne of Glory,
Cloath'd with white Robes, more splendid than th (Beams
That from the blazing Sun, at mid-day streams,
Whose blessed hands, such conquering Trophies bear,
As in the Roman Charriots, never were,

That on the Paradisian Banks repose,
Where living streams of Pleasure always flows,
Basking their souls, in those Immortal Rayes,
Which Everlasting Glory, there displays,
Thou'lt find their number so far to arise,
As no man's able to Arithmetize:
Those Saints that with Seraphick Angels join,
In Heavenly consort with their tunes Divine,
To sing forth that same great Doxology,
They are in number nigh Infinitie.

And that the poor, the Gospel do receive,
It shews his greatness, whom they do believe;
He that of nothing Heaven and Earth did raise,
From things that are not, still creates his paise;
And as in Power, so is he great in Grace,
That doth the mean despised ones embrace.

Whil'st men of note, through pride are apt to stray,
Thinking themselves too great for *Wisdom*'s Way:
But as the Mountains, whose high heads do shove
Unto the Lofty Clouds, do barren prove,
Whil'st the Low Valleys and stream wat'red Fields,
Their Loaded Crops, and fruitful burdens yield,
So with the Great, and Proud ones, doth it fare,
Whom God resists, whil'st Low ones blessed are;
That all the Glory might to him redound,
That doth by weak things, Mighty things confound.

Yet some for Honour, Wisdom, Power, fam'd,
Both in Divine, and humane records nam'd,

For Birth, and Wealth, for Arts, and Arms renoun'd,
Have in the tract of *Wifdoms* ways been found;
Whofe raifed Spirits, there did find, and know,
They had in truth, what once was but in fhow.

   Would'ft thou be *Noble?* *Wifdoms* ways then love,
They nobleft are, whofe birth is from above;
Who for their Creft, a Crown of Glory bear,
Upon a head, that doth to Heaven rear.

   Would'ft thou be *Wife?* there's none fo wife as thofe
That with the great, and chiefeft Good, do clofe;
That skilfully upon thofe means attend,
That do direct their fouls unto that end.

   Would'ft thou be *Great?* no Princes greater are
Than thofe that wreftle and prevail in Pray'r;
That conquer felf, and overcome in Fight
The Principalities and Powers of Might.
They mightier are that over Luft prevail,
Than thofe that do the ftrongeft Cities fcale.   (pat

   Would'ft thou be *Rich?* then come and tread thi
No Souls are Richer than the Rich in Faith:
Whofe large Revenew take it thus in Sum,
All good things prefent, all great things to come.

  Youth. Lady, excufe me till another day,
There's time enough hereafter for this way;
Let me my youthful daies pleafe in their choice,
And then I'll promife to obey thy *Voice*,
When *Age* hath quencht within this luftful fire,
And fhall in private weary limbs retire;

                            T

This will a season be to bend my mind,
Unto those ways where I may *Wisdom* find.

   Wisd. Vain *Youth*, vain *Youth*, hereafter is not thine,
He that hath now *no* heart, may have *no* time.
That Captain which to day doth terms afford,
May storm to morrow, and put all to'th' Sword;
And he that this day will not spread his sayl,
To morrow, if he would, may find no gale:
Or he that gives Grace to the penitent,
May not *Repentance* give to th' negligent.
But wilt thou in old *Age* these ways embrace?
Are weary limbs fit for to run a race?
And when the day is ready to shut in,
Is that a time this Great work to begin?
Shall *Satan* be presented with the prime,
And *Wisdom* only have the Dregs of Time?
Shall *Strength* and *Vigour*, be at his command?
At hers, a *Crazy* head, and *Palsey* hand?
Wilt thou keep back the sound from hallow'd flame,
And for oblation bring the blind and lame?
Do'st think it fit thy *Maker* should accept,
That which with scorn, thy *Ruler* would reject?

   In depth of *Winter*, when the Heavens are spred
With a black Vail, and all lights darkened;
When Clouds do thick return after the rain,
And their repeated showers pour down amain;
When that Tempestuous *Storms* beat round about,
Is this the only *Season* to set out?

                                   Surely,

Surely, if serious, this thou wilt not say,
VVhy is it then, vain *Youth*, thou would'st delay?
Oh that there were within thee once a heart,
From all the ways of *Folly* to depart!
Those *gaudy things* with which she takes thine eye,
Thou wilt be sure to find but *Vanity*.

  Youth. The *Wiseman*, though he said so, yet would try
Before he did believe it; so will I.

  Wisdom. But having try'd it, he hath fix'd a *Buoy*,
That others might not here themselves destroy.
His own *Experience* he hangs out for light,
That thou may'st see to steer thy way aright;
He sets a mark upon this dangerous shoal,
That upon it thou might'st not wrack thy Soul.
By Cautions, VVarnings, Tears, and sad Remorse,
He shews the *Hazard* of this *woful* course.
If after all this, when that thou hast seen
Those tops of *Masts* where sad Shipwrack hath been,
Yet thou will venture foolishly to stray,
Though *he* was spar'd, *thou* maist be cast away.
But should'st *thou* spared be, it hard would prove,
Fast rooted *habits* ever to remove:
For like the *Leopards* spots, and *Negro's* skin,
So *Custom* proveth in a way of sin.

  Youth. VVell, trouble me no more, I must fulfill
Those strong propensions that are in my *Will*.

  Wisd. And wilt thou rush, vain *Youth*, without all fea
Like to the Horse, upon the charged Spear?

Youths Tragedy. 13

Is Life a Trifle? Is a Future state
Not worth the caring for? and wilt thou hate
Thy precious *Soul*? wilt thou inhumane be
Unto thy self? oh, wretched *Crueltie*!
Wilt thou the way of *Folly* now pursue,
And turn thy back on *Wisdom*? then adieu.
But let me tell thee, that another day
Her path thou'lt find, like the *Strange Womans* way,
Who cometh forth with Smiles, in rich attire,
And with her kisses *Youthful Lust* doth fire:
In her curl'd Tresses *Lethal Nets* do lie,
And from her *Eye-lids* killing Darts do fly;
Between her breasts surprizing *Snares* abide,
Under her *Beauty* Deadly *Vipers* hide.
With honey strains her subtile lips do court
The *Simple* one, to her destructive sport;
With speeches smoother than the finest *Oyl*,
She doth betray into her fatal *Toyl*.
By wanton, amorous glances, she allures,
And with embracing arms her prey secures.
Thus by her flattering ways the Captives led,
Without all fear, to her perfumed bed,
Not thinking that her woful Guests do dwell
Within *Death*'s chambers, and the vaults of H...
But when a stranger's filled with his wealth,
And when he hath consumed all his health,
When that his *Honor*, and his *Labour* lies
Within her house, a slaughter'd *Sacrifice*,

When

When *Rottenness* enters into his bones,
And fills his flesh with pain, his breast with groans;
How doth he deeply now reflect upon
Those years, he gave unto the cruel one!
How doth he find that burning *Coals* he plac'd
Within his bosome, whil'st he her embrac'd!
How doth he now from his *Experience* cry,
He like a Bird, unto the *Snare* did fly!
And whil'st unto her way his steps he bent,
He, like an *Ox* unto the slaughter went;
And that same pleasure which he did so like,
Now, as a dart, doth through his Liver strike.
This is the way of *Folly*, this the end,
Her Feet to *Death*, her steps to *Hell* do tend. (glide
Like to those streams which through green Meadows
Till in the *Dead Sea* they at last do slide;
So runs her Course; through *Pleasure* though it take,
It ends in *Judgment*, and a fiery *Lake*.
Young Man, farewel, oh, mind thy future state,
Take Counsel now, before it be too late.
Oh now remember those invited *Guests*,
That being call'd slighted the Marriage Feast:
But for so great contempt did dearly pay;
Where *Mercy* could not gain, there *Wrath* did slay.

YOUTH.

What strange *Impressions* do my Spirits feel?
How do my former *Resolutions* reel?

What

Youths Tragedy.

What strange *Convulsions* seize upon my Mind?
What inward quick *Distortions* do I find?
How do my *Thoughts* press forth on every side;
And in two great *Battalia's* do divide;
Assaulting each the other with great Force,
Sometimes *Lust* gaining Ground, sometimes *Remorse*:
With armed troops, the *Sensual Appetite*
Doth beat down all before it in the Fight,
Till *Conscience* with fresh succours doth oppose,
And, by strong hand, her Forces overthrows.
Affections see it, and do haste to bring
Relief and Succour to the broken *Wing*:
And so with furious rage, they down do fell
All that their fierce *Impressions* would repell;
The *Will* well backed with the chiefest flower
Of *Veteran* Soldiers, with a mighty power
Doth on the Gross of the *Battalia* fall,
And questions not but for to carry all.
And now the *Judgment* with its utmost might
Makes strong resistance, and prevents a flight;
And with brave *Courage*, and repeated blows,
Represseth the great fury of her Foes.
And whil'st they thus engage with Warlike hands,
Victoria now between them doubtful stands.

This is the *War* that gives my Mind no rest,
My *Judgment* tells me *Wisdoms* wayes are best:
My *Conscience* checks me that I don't obey,
And shews the *danger*, if I do delay.

My *Will*, and my *Affections* do oppose,
And would with *Sensual pleasures* have me close:
Thus in sad Fears and Cares my thoughts do roul,
Whil'st that I have these workings in my Soul.
What I shall do, I know not; this I find,
That strong *Convictions* do assault my Mind.

    The *Devil*, *Youth*, and the *Nuncius*.

5.   *Devil*. *Youth*, What's the matter, wilt thou quit the
And to a Melancholy *Fancy* yield? (field,
Wilt thou expose thy self to taunting *Jears*,
Whil'st thus thou load'st thy breast with needless fears?
Go fill thy hand, and head with those affairs,
That this *World* calls for, and so choak these cares:
Or take thy *Pastime* at some pleasant *Play*,
And with those streins of *Wit* drive *Fear* away:
With *Scenes* and Objects go and feast thine *Eyes*,
And glut thy *Lusts* with great Varieties.
Or, to thy old Companions straight resort,
And so divert thy self with *Youthful Sport*.
Go pierce the choicest *Liquors*, and drink down
Full draughts thereof, till thou these *Troubles* drown:
Or joyn thy self unto the Jovial Blades,
Who hunt forth *Pleasures*, in their *Maskarades*.
Let those Cross-workings that thy *Soul* doth meet,
Be prostrate laid at some fair *Ladies* feet.
Why should thy day be stained with a Cloud,
And all thy comforts under Darkness shroud?

                                Nun.

Nun. The Young man listens first, and then revolves
The Pleasure offer'd, and at last resolves
To make a trial; thus his feet are led
Into those Paths that wind unto the dead.
Like unto him, that views the sparkling *Wine*
That doth in Crimson Robe through Crystal shine,
And is delighted, whil'st he doth survey
Its Jocund *Spirits*, on the top to play;
Until at length, seduced by his look,
He baiteth for himself a deadly hook,
And swallows down that which at last doth bring
The *Serpents* biting teeth, and *Adders* sting;
So whil'st the Young man with Temptation plays,
And on Gilt out-sides wantonly doth gaze,
He in the Paths of Folly soon doth stray,
And to *Satanick Wiles*, becomes a prey,
Who forward still, his Captive doth ingage,
Hur'ing him though, many a dirty Stage:
For whil'st in *Pleasure*, he his Soul doth drench,
All his *Convictions* he at last doth quench,
And like the Dog that doth by th' Anvil lie,
About whose ears, hot sparks from loud blows flie.
Which at the first, he could no way endure,
But now by use he comes to sleep secure;
So sleeps this *Youth*, the Terrour once in sin
Being extinguish'd, through a course therein.
And so his Heart grows hard, his *Conscience* sear'd;
And now he mocks at that which once he fear'd;

From frequent *Acts*, he comes for to *Devise*
That against which, at first, his heart did rise.
(He that will venture on a way of sin,
Many a dreadful step may take therein.)
His Time it is but short, for you may see
In the next *Scenes* his sad *Catastrophe*.

Youth.

*cen.*6.   *Youth*. How do I now in Pleasures bosom rest,
Whil'st Checks and Fears are banish'd from my breast!
Those *Menaces* that on my *Thoughts* did throng,
I have repuls'd; the threat'ned man lives long;
Is not this better than to whine away,
With pensive, pewling *Mopes*, my pleasant day?
How joyful is it now unto my sight,
To see my self adrift in all delight?
And as this is a day of mirth to me,
So shall to morrow more abundant be.

Nuncius.

*Scen.*7.   *Nun*. So *Foolish* and so *Vain* a thing is Man,
Whose *Joyes* are *Bubbles*, and whose *Life's* a *Span*;
Yet for to promise both he is so mad,
As if the *Royalty* of both he had.
But like the *Poste* that swiftly passeth by,
Or like the *Slave* that doth from bondage fly,
Or like a nimble *Ship*, that with full sayl
Doth run her course before a prosperous gale;

Or

Or like the *Eagle* that her Prey espies,
Like *Lightning*, with swift wings unto it flies;
So *Time* now speeds to let the *Young Man* know
That all his way and walks are a *vain show*.

Time and *Youth*.

Time. With winged swiftness I do hither flie,
To let *thee* know thy *fatal end* draws nigh.
Like to the Grass, or like the fading Flower,
So withereth all thy Glory in an hour:
Too late *Experience* now must teach *thee* this,
Thy *life* a *Shadow* and a *Vapour* is.
I shall no more turn thy neglected Glass;
A few *sands* only now remain to pass;
My whetted *Sythe* comes next for to be us'd,
To let thee know, *Time* will not be abus'd.

Youth. My *Aged Father*, turn thy *Sythe* away,
Cut down the ripened *Ears*, let green ones stay;
Go where the Fields are white, whose stalks do bend,
Under their burden, and there put an end
Unto those pressures, but with-hold thy hand
From the green *Blades*; let immature ones stand.
I am too young yet for the *Sythe* of *Time*,
Come when my *Locks* shall be as *white* as *thine*.

Time. Forbear, fond *Youth*, *Time*'s not at thy com-
The tender bud oft feels my cropping hand; (mand,
Hast thou not often read *Elegiack* Verse,
Compos'd to celebrate a *Virgin* Herse?

Hast

Haſt thou not ſeen the Mother, with wet eyes,
Sprinkle the duſt wherein her *Young Son* lies;
How oft hath *Death* white *Trophies* to declare,
Thoſe he leads captive forth, they *young ones* are?
I know where lies my work, advice pray ſpare,
Where I ſhould reap, and where I ſhould forbear;
I count thy *Sands*, and when the laſt I ſee
Fly to its *heap*, thou'rt ripe enough for me.

  Youth. Much honour'd Father, let my ſuit prevail,
O're look my boldneſs, pardon where I fail.

  Time. How much I've honor'd been, thou know'ſt full well,
Thy waſted *Days*, and reveling *Nights* can tell,
Wherein thy great contempt was ſhew'n that durſt
Make me a *Paſtime* to thy bruitiſh *Luſt*.
Yet blame not me, thy *Sands* ſo ſoon did paſs,
But blame thoſe *Luſts* that often Jog'd thy Glaſs.

  Youth. Yet once more *Father*, let thy gentle hand
Give longer *Date* unto my fleeting *Sand*;
I've waſted much, what now thy bounty lends,
I'le only ſpend to make thy ſelf amends.

  Time. Thoſe *Purpoſes*, that ſudden *Fear* doth raiſe,
Too often prove like to a thorny blaze.
When ſtrugling ſtorms from ſtraitning Caverns rend,
And Flame-torn Clouds, their thundring Showrs down ſend,
When ſwelling *Floods*, with angry *Voice* do roar,
And ſend their *Wracks*, to beat the ſtubborn *Shoar*,
How doth the Frightned Sea-man fall to pray'r
And with large Vows, his hands to Heaven rear,

                                  Whil'ſt

Whil'ft the fierce ftroke of ev'ry raging *Wave*,
Threatens to make, the fwallowing deep his *Grave*;
When as no fooner, are his Feet on Shore,
But he's as bad, or worfer than before.
So tumble down thofe high rais'd Vows, whofe *Bafe*
Are not fure founded on renewing *Grace*.
Time will not truft thee, look thy Glafs is broke;
And *Death* comes now, to give the *Fatal ftroke*.

Death, **Nuncius**, and *Youth*.

Death. *Youth*, come away, for thou muft with me go
To the dark *Regions* that do lie below;
Come, this fame hand muft feize upon thy breath,
And lead thee down into the fhades of *Death*.
Here is no dwelling for thee, but thou muft
Take up thy lodging with me in the *Duft*;
And in thick *Darknefs* make thy difmal bed,
Whil'ft crawling *Worms* under thy head are fpread;
The pleafant *light* no more thine *Eyes* fhall fee,
But with *Corruption* thou muft cover'd be.
Thofe thoughts that are gone forth for to purvey
To Feaft thy *Lufts* in this thy youthful day;
And all thofe pleafing *Hopes* thou didft fo cherifh,
Of long continued *Blifs*, muft this day perifh.

Nun. Whil'ft that the *Youth* the King of *Terrours*
His trembling limbs a *cold fweat* all bedews, (views
His Pulfe beats quick, his gaftly Face looks pale,
His fpirits fink, and his ftout heart doth fail;

As

As when *Defendants* from out-works are beat,
They to their main strength make a swift retreat,
That, by united Force, they may oppose
The fierce attempts of their approaching *Foes*;
So to the Heart, his scattered Forces flow,
That there they may keep off the *fatal blow*;
But when this will not do, a parley's beat,
And now his Enemy he begins to treat.

Youth. Oh *Death*, forbear me, but a little while,
Until my *Vessel* I provide with *Oyl*;
I am not yet prepared with a *Light*
To comfort me in this same dismal *Night*.
Let not my *Feet* on the dark *Mountains* fall
For lack of *Light* to guide my steps withall.
Oh, let my *naked Soul* put on her *Vest*,
Why should I fare like the *unwelcome Guest*?
In stormy weather pull not down my Tent
Before I have a better Tenement.
Oh let me stay, that I may make a *Friend*,
For to receive me at my *Journeys* end.
Oh let me truly *Live*, before I *Die*,
I want Provision for *Eternitie*.

Death. Vain *Youth*, already thou hast had thy *Day*
But *Grace* was slighted, *Time* was sinn'd away.
Could nothing waken but the *Mid-Night* Cry
For to provide, when 'tis too late to buy?
Is it a time thy *Naked Soul* to dress,
When that the *King* is come to *view* his *Guess*?

Ha

Hast thou a Habitation still neglected,
Until the *hour* thou com'st to be ejected?
When thou art *Harbourless*, and Storms begin,
Hast thou a *Friend* to seek to take thee in?
Ah, careless *Soul!* how woful is thy *state*,
That know'st not how to want, or I to wait!
Come, come away, I am not sent to treat,
But for to bring thee to the *Judgment Seat*.

Nun. Whil'st Death to strike lifts up his *Fatal hand*,
And *Friends* about, with helpless tears do stand;
His Rowling Eyes, for aid unto them turn,
But all in vain, Alas they can but mourn!
And now his quivering hands begin to catch,
As if from *Death*, his mortal Dart they'd snatch.

But like the Flame of an expiring Lamp,
That for to save it self from gloomy damp,
Seeks the exhausted Oyl with catching light,
Which when it finds not, vanisheth into Night;
So doth his perishing Life strive to maintain
Its lingring being, but 'tis all in Vain.
What stay he gains, serves only to present
The following Terrour which he thus doth Vent.

Youth. How shall I now appear before that *Face*
That rends the *Rocks*, and *Mountains* doth displace;
That melts the *Hills*, and makes the *Earth* to quake;
That flings down *Stars*, and doth the *Heavens* shake;
That makes those vast expansions for to roul,
And shrink themselves together, like a scroul?

D How

How shall I stand before that dreadful *Throne*,
From whence bright *Lightnings* and great *Thundrings* come?
How shall my guilty *Soul*, endure to hear
That Voice, that doth the Lofty Cedars tear,
From which hot burning Coals, and Hail-stones fly
With hideous noise rending the troubled Sky?
The *Channels* of the *Frightned Deep* lie bare,
The *Pillars* of the *Trembling World* appear?
Who can abide the *Fierceneß* of his *Ire*,
Whose *indignation's* poured out like *Fire*?

Nun. But go he must; *Death* pierc'd his tender side,
And in his Heart blood his bright Dart he dy'd.
Out flies the trembling *Soul*, a Guard doth hale
It to that Court admitteth of no Bayle.
Her *Mittimus* is drawn, she's sent away,
To lie in Prison till the *Judgment* Day.
Let's lay our ears unto the *Doleful Pit*,
And hearken there what doth become of it.

The *Soul* and the *Devil*.

Soul. Deceitful *Devil*, Wilt thou now *torment*
That *Soul*, thou lately flatt'redst with *Content*?
Are all those Promises thou mad'st of *Bliß*,
And futur *Glory*, are they come to this?

Devil. My Promises, vain *Soul*, they were mistook,
I us'd them but as Baits to hide my *Hook*;
My end's accomplish'd, I the prey have caught,
And now I'le use thee as my *Captives* ought;

With

With Chains of *Darkneß* I must bind thee fast,
And in these *Flames* of *Wrath* I must thee cast.

  Soul. O wretched *Soul!* how hast thou lost that place
Where *Saints* and *Angels* do behold the *Face*
Of Everlasting *Glory*, and do sing
Eternal *Hallelujahs* to their *King* :
Upon whose Heads are Crowns of *Glory* worn,
And by whose hands *Triumphant Palmes* are born :
Who in the *Bosom* of dear *Love* do rest,
And on the purest *Joyes* for ever feast ;
Whil'st with the *Damned Spirits* I do make
My habitation in this *Firy Lake* ;
The Flaming *Pile* whereof is kindled by
The *Breath* of that incensed *Majesty*,
Which like a stream of *Brimstone*, where it runs,
All things before it into *Fire* turns.

  Oh dismal place ! where *Vollies* of *Outcries*,
And hideous *Howlings* like to *Thunder* flies.
The *horrid noise*, and dreadful *shrieks* that came
From the *Philistines*, when that massy *Frame*,
Bereft of both its *Pillars* down did fall,
And into *Death* and *Ruin* crusht them all ;
The frightful *Roarings* and the woful *Cries*,
Which *Sodom* sent unto the *Angry Skies*,
Whil'st on their wicked heads they forth did pour
(Of *Fire* and *Brimstone*) a consuming shower ;
Are instances too short for to declare
Those *Wailings* that among the *Damned* are.

Oh Woful State! their *Torments* who can tell,
That with *Devouring Fire* for ever dwell?
The *Wracking Wheel*, on which the *Bones* are broke,
By a most gradual and deliberate stroke;
The *Firy Pinchers*, which deep *Wounds* do tear,
That *scalding Sulphur* may be poured there;
The *Stripes* of *Scorpions*, that long Furrows make,
With cutting *Saws* that through the *Marrow* rake:
The Stings of *Dragons*, and the rending Claws
Of rav'nous *Lions*, for their hungry Jaws;
The *Cauldrons* that with Plumbean liquor boil,
The *Gridir'ns* whereon *living Flesh* doth broil;
With thousands of like *Tortures* do not bear
Proportion to the *Torments* that are here:
And yet this is the Portion of my *Soul*,
Which now is like that dreadful, bitter *Roul*,
Fill'd full with *Lamentations*, *Mournings*, *Woes*,
And floods of *Wrath*, which from *Dire Vengeance* flows.

Horrid *Reflections* likewise do I find,
Adding great *Anguish* to my *Tortur'd Mind*.
Whil'st I consider that for *empty Toyes*,
I have for ever lost *substantial Joyes*;
And whil'st I think how oft I have rejected;
That Counsel which to *Peace* my steps directed;
How oft I have extinguish'd that same light
Which *Conscience* brought to guide my feet aright;
How all my precious *Time* I vainly spent,
And now no *Time* is left for to *Repent*:

This

This like a dreadful *Worm* doth ever gnaw
Upon my *Vitals* with infatiate *Maw*.
  Oh now that *Death*, which late my heart-ftrings
Would come and eafe me by a deeper ftroke! (broke,
Oh, how I would as a fweet *Cordial* rate
That blow which fhould this *Soul Annihilate*!
If fuch a wifh but granted I might have,
I would account that hand that *kill'd*, did *fave*.
Oh, this would *Mercy* prove, but none remains,
Not the leaft drop to cool me in thefe *Flames*.
I now muft Dying live and Living dye,
Scorch'd in thefe *Flames* to all *Eternity*.

Nuncius.

Sc. II

Let us withdraw our Ears from this fad place,
And liften now unto the Call of *Grace*.
Hark how the Angels do proclaim and fing
Peace upon *Earth*, and *Glory* to that *King*
Who in the higheft *Heavens* hath his *Throne*,
And towards men his good will maketh known.
  See now, how many pleafant Feet there are
Upon our *Mountains* that glad tidings bear
Of the bright *Day-fpring*, Shining from on high,
To lighten thofe, who in *Death's* fhades do lie;
And to direct our wandring feet aright,
Out of black darknefs, to the paths of light.
  Behold how *Wifdom* lifteth up her cry
Within our Gates, and where fhe doth efpy

The thickest *Concourse*, and the greatest *Throng*,
There she invites with her mellifluous Tongue,
That all unto her *Palace* would repare,
And of her dainties take a liberal share.

 That *Persian King* whose Scepter gave commands
From Indian streams, to Æthiopian sands;
Before whose peaceful *Throne*, and Crowned brow,
The mighty *Powers* of th' Orient World did bow;
That from the purvey'd Elements, had stor'd
With Princely dainties, his most Royal board,
And entertain'd his Nobles, with such fare,
As might his *Glory*, to the World declare;
Had no such banquet, as is here sent in,
From the rich Love, of *Heaven*, and *Earth*'s great *King*:
That perish'd in the using, but in this
Eternal life's serv'd up in every dish.

 Look how awak'ned *Souls* shake off the bands
Of dismal Darkness, and the proud commands
Of the *Æthereal Powers* at *Wisdoms* cry,
And like the Doves unto her windows fly,
Where *Mercy* ready stands, to wellcome all
That yield obedience to her blessed Call:
Scorners, and *Fools*, yea such as long have bin
Bewilder'd in the crooked *Ways* of Sin,
If they return, *Mercy* will them embrace
In tender Arms, of Everlasting Grace.

 Th' ungrateful Son that did his Father leave,
From whose free hand, he largely did receive

A

Youths Tragedy.

A liberal portion, which he vainly spent
On swinish Lusts, and sordid merriment,
And wander'd far; until for want of bread
The *Swine* he kept, and with the *Swine* he fed:
No sooner did this hungry *Prodigal*,
From wandring steps, his weary feet recall,
And from the barren *Waste*, doth bend his course
Unto his Father's house, with true Remorse;
But like the golden Beams of dawning light
Unto the *Watchman*, tir'd with stormy night,
Which do no sooner from the Orient dart,
But they are wellcom'd, with a chearful heart,
So is the sight of this returning Son,
Whose Father, to him, yet far off, doth run;
Embraceth, kisseth, cloatheth with the best,
And entertains him with a joyful Feast.

   Only presume not, but without delay
Close with the voice of *Wisdom*, now to day:
Though it's a truth, that always here bears date,
That true Repentance, never comes too late;
Yet thou wilt find it, upon serious view,
That Late Repentance, seldom proveth true.

   But grant it real prove, how great a time
Is spent in eating Husks, and feeding Swine;
In which thy empty Soul might have been fed
With Angels Food, and with the Childrens bread?
How long a bondage dost thou undergo,
Worse than the Slave, that doth in Gally row?

Or his, whom *Caphtor*'s sons in chains did bind,
Thrust in a Mill, with Eyes thrust out, to grind.
Whom Satan, at his will doth captive lead,
And every sordid lust doth on thee tread;
That might long since, such *Freedom* have possest,
As doth the Denizons of Heaven invest:
How art thou doing that, which if once won
To Paths of life, with tears must be undone;
Wasting that Time which might fit many a Gem
With pollish'd Lustre, for thy Diadem.

   Then gird thy Morning loins, to spend thy days
In working here, for thy *Creator*'s praise,
Who with propitious Eye, will have regard
Unto thy pains to give a full reward.

The Epilogue.

The end, is endless, Wisdoms ways in Bliss,
The Paths of Folly, *in the great* A-byss,
Wherein Grace-slighting Youth, ingulft remains,
To spend an endless Now, *in Direful flames:*
Be caution'd then, For he that will not take
Example now, shall an Example make.

FINIS.

D
S 3393

147750

REPRODUCED FROM THE COPY IN THE

HENRY E. HUNTINGTON LIBRARY

FOR REFERENCE ONLY, NOT FOR REPRODUCTION